Creepy Creatures

WELDON OWEN PTY LTD
Chairman: John Owen
Publisher: Sheena Coupe
Associate Publisher: Lynn Humphries
Managing Editor: Helen Bateman
Design Concept: Sue Rawkins
Senior Designer: Kylie Mulquin
Production Manager: Caroline Webber
Production Assistant: Kylie Lawson

Text: Sharon Dalgleish
Consultant: George McKay, Conservation Biologist
U.S. Editors: Laura Cavaluzzo and Rebecca McEwen

08 07 06 05 04
10 9 8 7 6 5

Published in the United States by
Wright Group/McGraw-Hill
One Prudential Plaza
Chicago IL 60601
www.WrightGroup.com

Printed in Singapore.
ISBN: 0-7699-0469-6
ISBN: 0-7699-0592-7 (6-pack)

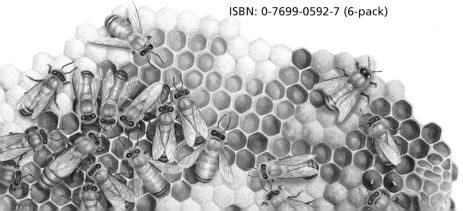

CONTENTS

INSPECTING INSECTS

There are more than a million species of insects. That's more kinds of insects than all the other animal species put together! Insects are very small, so they need only tiny amounts of food, and they can live in very cramped spaces. They can also survive tough conditions that would be too hot or too cold for other animals.

DID YOU KNOW?

A silverfish has such a flat body that it can wriggle between the pages of a book!

Head
This is one of the strongest parts of the body.

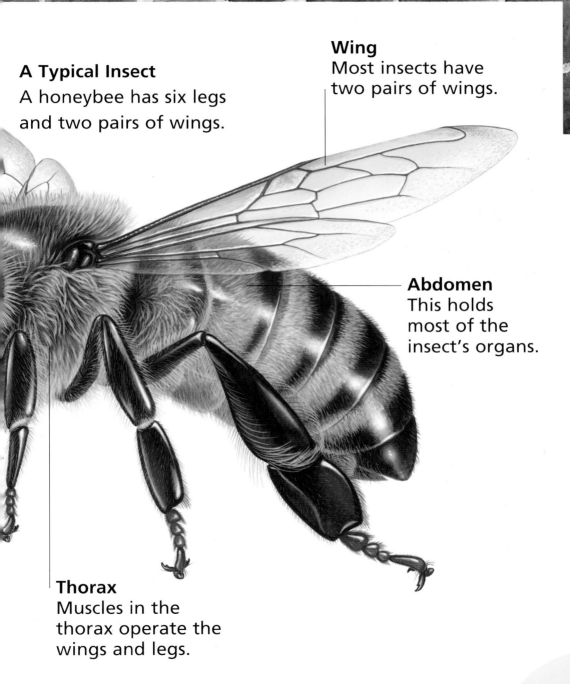

Wing
Most insects have
two pairs of wings.

A Typical Insect
A honeybee has six legs
and two pairs of wings.

Abdomen
This holds
most of the
insect's organs.

Thorax
Muscles in the
thorax operate the
wings and legs.

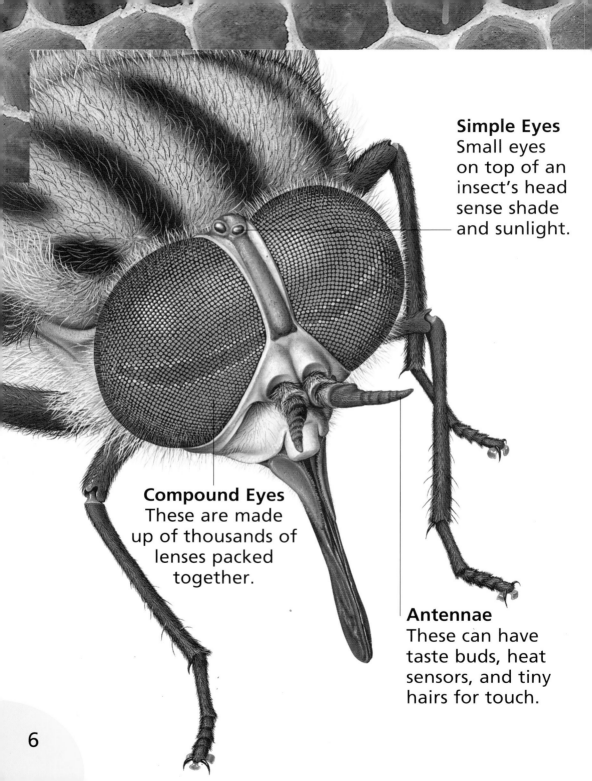

Simple Eyes
Small eyes on top of an insect's head sense shade and sunlight.

Compound Eyes
These are made up of thousands of lenses packed together.

Antennae
These can have taste buds, heat sensors, and tiny hairs for touch.

6

SENSING THE WORLD

Like many other animals, insects have five main senses—sight, hearing, smell, touch, and taste. Different insects use some senses more than others. Dragonflies fly during the day, so they have large eyes. Most moths fly at night. In the darkness, they use smell more than sight.

I CAN HEAR YOU

Some insects, like the grasshopper, have ears on their body. A lacewing can sense movement with its thin wings. Ants sense movement through their legs.

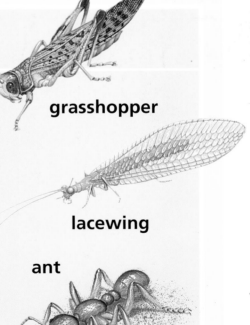

grasshopper

lacewing

ant

HUNGRY HUNTERS

Some insects are active hunters. Tiger beetles can run half a yard in a second to catch ants for their dinner. Other insects lie in wait until food comes within reach. They are often well camouflaged to match their environment. Not all insects are hunters. Some are parasites. They live on or in another animal and feed on its body or blood.

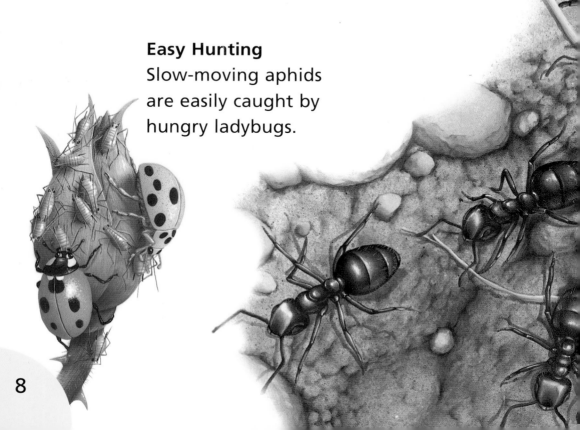

Easy Hunting
Slow-moving aphids are easily caught by hungry ladybugs.

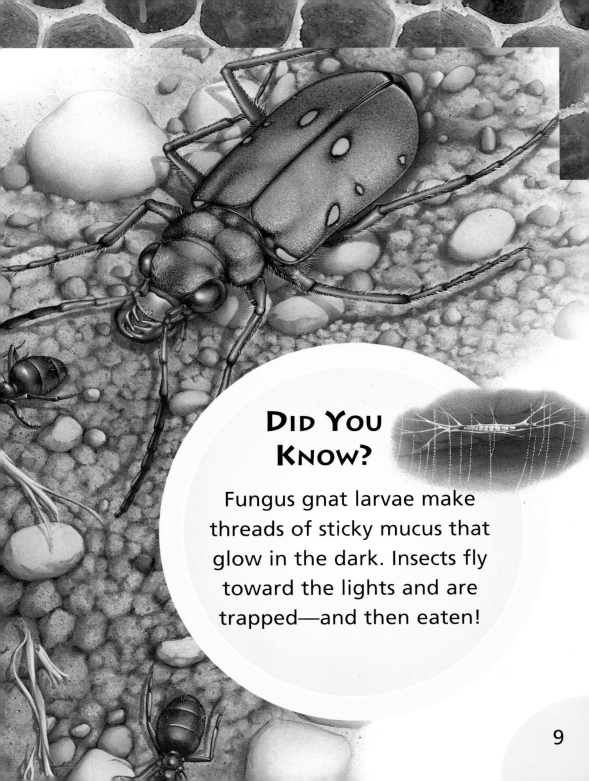

DID YOU KNOW?

Fungus gnat larvae make threads of sticky mucus that glow in the dark. Insects fly toward the lights and are trapped—and then eaten!

FLYING HIGH

Most insects have two pairs of wings. They can fly away quickly to escape danger, and they can hover in the air while searching for food. A ladybug's back wings are packed away under its hard front wings. When it wants to fly away, it has to open its front wings, unfold its back wings, then beat its back wings fast enough to take off.

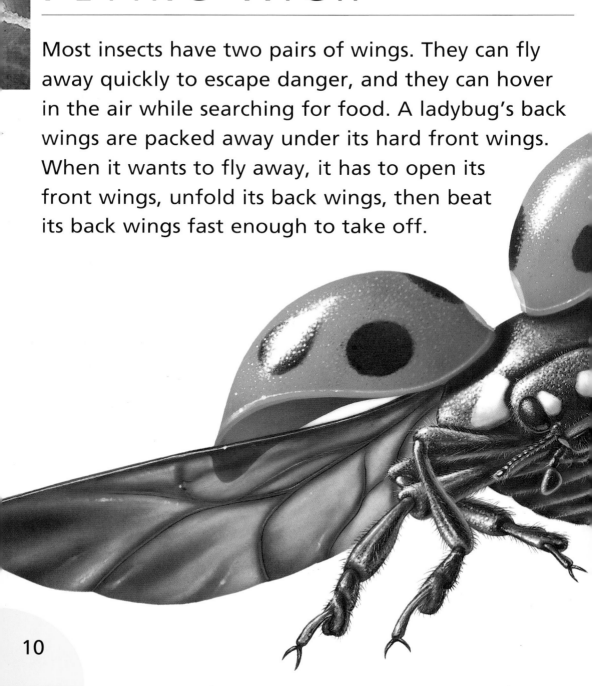

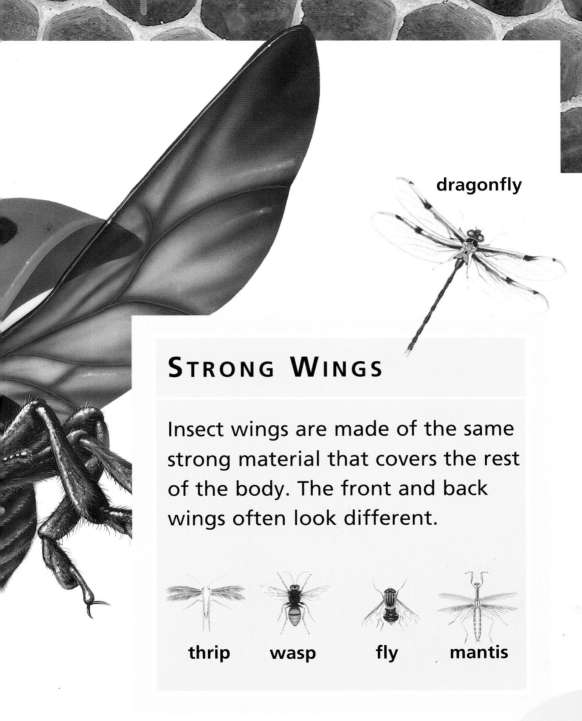

dragonfly

STRONG WINGS

Insect wings are made of the same strong material that covers the rest of the body. The front and back wings often look different.

thrip   **wasp**   **fly**   **mantis**

Escape Artist

When a click beetle is in danger, it lies on its back and pretends to be dead. When the danger passes, it snaps its head upward so that it lands on its feet.

MOVING AROUND

Insects weigh so little, they can stop and start far more suddenly than we can—which sometimes gives people a fright! Most adult insects move using their legs. They walk or run, or even jump into the air. Grasshoppers are champion jumpers. They have springlike joints in their knees, and powerful back legs to launch themselves into the air.

DID YOU KNOW?

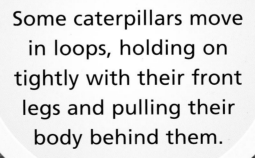

Some caterpillars move in loops, holding on tightly with their front legs and pulling their body behind them.

BIZARRE BEETLES

Over millions of years, beetles have evolved into strange shapes and different sizes. The largest beetle is the Hercules beetle from Central America, which can grow to nearly 8 inches (20 centimeters) long. The smallest is the feather-winged beetle. It's so small it looks like a tiny dot! All beetles have hard front wings that fit over the back wings to keep them safe.

DID YOU KNOW?

Whirligig beetles make ripples on water that bounce back and tell them where to find food.

Harlequin Beetle
This beetle feeds at night. It has long antennae.

DON'T EAT ME!

The bright colors of ladybug beetles warn enemies that they have a bitter taste.

five-spotted ladybug

ten-spotted ladybug

Tortoise Beetle
With its flat thorax, the tortoise beetle looks like a coin.

Giraffe Weevil
This beetle has a long head and a slim thorax.

Larva
The caterpillar
hatches from an egg.

Pupa
The pupa is covered
by a tough case.

GROWING UP

Butterflies and moths begin as eggs, which hatch into caterpillars. The main job of a caterpillar, or larva, is to eat and grow. When a larva is big enough, it rests as a pupa, slowly changing shape and growing wings. Butterflies are colorful and fly by day, while most moths are dull and fly at night.

Airborne
The adult moth breaks out of the case.

moth

Opening Up
The larva's body breaks down and changes.

butterfly

DID YOU KNOW?

Butterflies rest with their wings upright. Moths rest with their wings held flat.

SOCIAL INSECTS

Most insects live alone. Ants and termites are different, and so are many species of bees and wasps. They live in family groups and share the work they need to do. In a beehive, the queen bee lays all the eggs. Her children are the workers who look after the nest, raise the young, and find food.

pollen stores

AMAZING!

Some beetles trick ants into taking them into their nest. Then they trick the ants into feeding them.

Open Larva Cell
Newly hatched larvae are fed by worker bees.

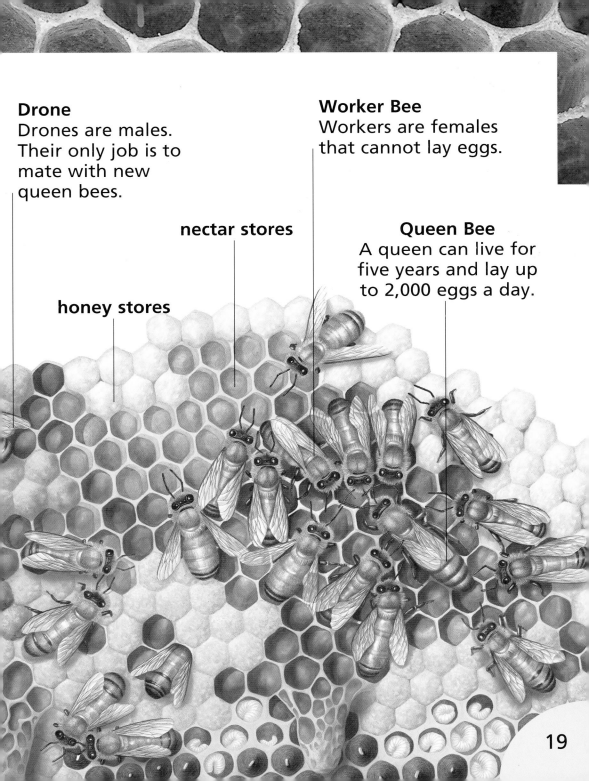

Drone
Drones are males. Their only job is to mate with new queen bees.

Worker Bee
Workers are females that cannot lay eggs.

nectar stores

honey stores

Queen Bee
A queen can live for five years and lay up to 2,000 eggs a day.

TRUE BUGS

People often call any kind of insect a bug, but true bugs are insects with mouths that stab and suck. Some bugs, such as aphids and cicadas, live on plants and drink the sap, which is rich in sugar. Other bugs attack the flesh of animals. Bedbugs hide during the day and feed on animal blood at night!

DID YOU KNOW?

If a stinkbug is in danger, it makes a terrible smell! Many are brightly colored to warn birds to stay away.

Sneak Attack
The back swimmer swims on its back, waiting to stab any insects that fall onto the water.

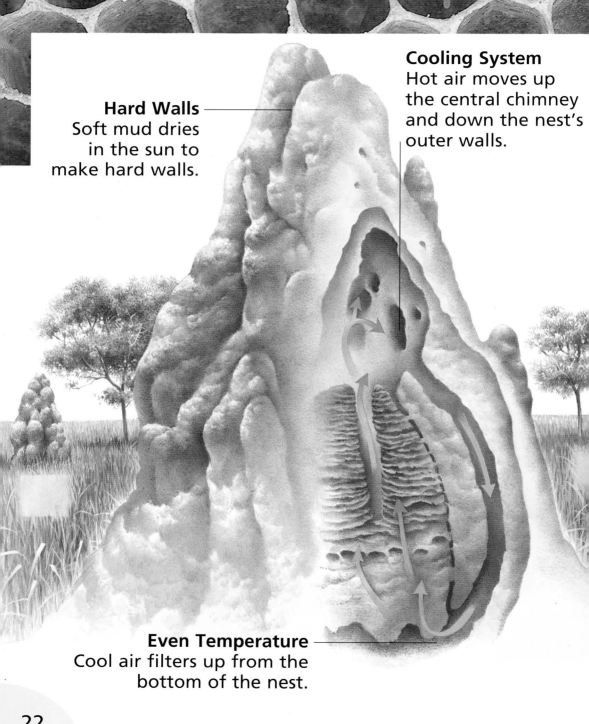

Hard Walls
Soft mud dries
in the sun to
make hard walls.

Cooling System
Hot air moves up
the central chimney
and down the nest's
outer walls.

Even Temperature
Cool air filters up from the
bottom of the nest.

MUDDY MOUNDS

Termites have specific roles in building nests. No one termite is in charge, but each builder knows exactly what to do. Some termite mounds are big enough to house millions of termites and can be more than 6½ yards (6 meters) high. Other nests are built high in trees and have sloping roofs to keep out the rain.

CLEVER BUILDERS

Magnetic termites build their mounds so that the flat sides face east and west. This way they avoid the midday heat.

SPIDERS

Spiders are not insects. All spiders have eight long legs and bulbous bodies divided into two parts. They have powerful jaws with fangs that can give a poisonous bite. A spider uses its venom to paralyze or kill its prey. Then it injects the prey with special juices that dissolve the tissue so the spider can slowly suck it up.

Claws
These are used to walk along silk threads.

Leg
A spider has eight legs.

Munching on the Side
A true spider's jaws are below its head and bite sideways.

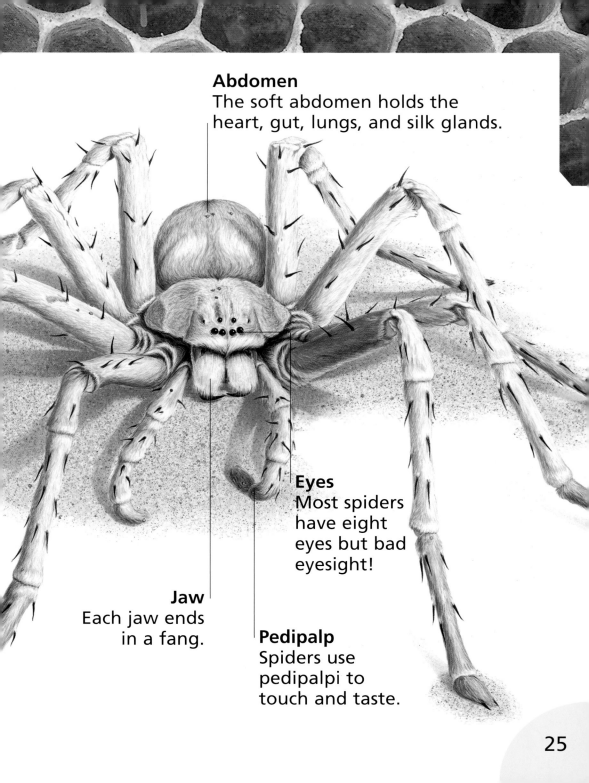

Abdomen
The soft abdomen holds the heart, gut, lungs, and silk glands.

Eyes
Most spiders have eight eyes but bad eyesight!

Jaw
Each jaw ends in a fang.

Pedipalp
Spiders use pedipalpi to touch and taste.

25

Spiders use silk to weave their webs. They make the silk in special glands in their abdomen. Silk starts as a liquid that hardens as the spider tugs at it with its legs. The strands can be stronger than steel. When a victim gets caught in a web, the spider wraps it in more sticky threads before giving it a deadly bite.

Sailing Away
Some young spiders use threads of silk to launch themselves into the wind and leave the nest.

Tailor-made Trap

You can tell the species of
spider by the shape of its
web. Orb weavers spin a
spiral of silk, covered with
sticky droplets. Triangle
spiders keep their web
tight until something lands
in it. Then they let it go
loose, so the prey will get
tangled. Sheet-web spiders
spin a maze of webs to
trap their prey. Most
spiders are quick to repair
any damage to their webs.

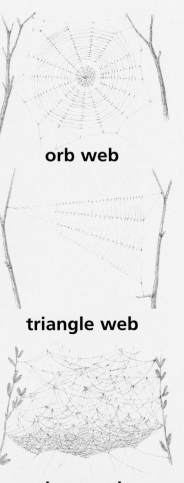

orb web

triangle web

sheet web

27

Not all spiders make webs. Some build clever traps, while others set off on patrol and pounce on prey. Spiders also have ways to outwit their enemies. Many use camouflage, blending in with their backgrounds. One spider looks like bird droppings! Some spiders hide in burrows and hold their trapdoors firmly shut until the danger passes.

The Great Escape
The Namibian wheel spider escapes danger by curling its legs and turning itself into a wheel. It can speed along at more than 3 feet (1 meter) per second.

Dinner for Two
Pitcher plants trap and digest insects. Crab spiders try to get to the insects first!

Stealing Dinner
This crab spider has built a web across the inside of the pitcher. Insects that tumble in will be caught in the web before reaching the water.

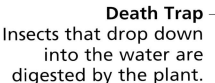

Death Trap
Insects that drop down into the water are digested by the plant.

29

GLOSSARY

camouflage Something in an animal's appearance that allows it to blend into its surroundings, so it can stay safe, or catch food.

evolved A description of a plant or animal whose body or habits have gradually changed in ways that allow it to live more successfully in its environment.

fangs Long, sharp teeth that spiders and snakes use to inject poison into their prey.

larva The early wormlike form of an insect, before it becomes a pupa.

pupa An insect that is at the noneating stage between being a larva and an adult.

venom Poison that is injected by certain animals to attack enemies, or by plants to trap food.

INDEX

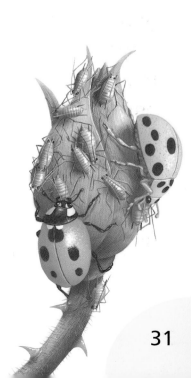

31

CREDITS AND NOTES

Picture and Illustration Credits
[t=top, b=bottom, l=left, r=right, c=center, F=front, B=back, C=cover, bg=background]
Susanna Addario 2b, 12bc, 13cr, 18–19br, 30tr, FClc.
Corel Corporation 20cl, 23br, 4–32 borders, Cbg. **Simone End** 1c, 14cl, 14bc, 15cl, 15br, 15cr, 15tr. **Christer Eriksson** 8bl, 10–11c, 12–13c, 31br, FCc. **Giuliano Fornari** 27rc, 27tr, 27br. **Jon Gittoes** 21c, 28–29bl, 29r. **Ray Grinaway** 3tr, 11br, 11cr, 11bl, 11bc. **Tim Hayward/Bernard Thornton Artists UK** 24cl, 26bc, FCtl. **Robert Hynes** 22c. **David Kirshner** 4cl, 4–5c. **Frank Knight** 16–17tc. **Barbara Rodanska** 18bl. **Trevor Ruth** 17bl, 17cr, BC. **Claudia Saraceni** 8–9c, 9cr. **Kevin Stead** 6c, 7br, 7c, 7cr. **Thomas Trojer** 24–25rc.

Acknowledgements
Weldon Owen would like to thank the following people for their assistance in the production of this book:
Jocelyne Best, Ivan Finnegan, Peta Gorman, Tracey Jackson, Andrew Kelly, Sarah Mattern, Emily Wood.